The Christian Horse

A man's lost and has been walking in the desert for days. He has just about lost all hope when he comes across the home of a missionary. The missionary kindly takes him in and nurses him back to health. Feeling better, the man asks the missionary for directions to the nearest town. On his way out the backdoor, he sees this horse. He goes back into the house and asks the missionary, "Could I borrow your horse and give it back when I reach the town?"

The missionary says, "Sure but there is a special thing about this horse. You have to say 'Thank God' to make it go and 'Amen' to make it stop."

Not paying much attention, the man says, "Sure, ok."

So he gets on the horse and says, "Thank God" and the horse starts walking. Then he says, "Thank God, thank God," and the horse starts trotting.

Feeling really brave, the man says, "Thank God, thank God, thank God, thank God, thank God" and the horse just takes off. Pretty soon he sees this cliff coming up and he's doing everything he can to make the horse stop.

"Whoa, stop, hold on!!!!"

Finally he remembers, "Amen!!"

The horse stops 4 inches from the cliff. Then the man leans back in the saddle, sighs and says,

"Thank God."

The Devil And The Lawyer

An attorney was sitting in his office late one night, when the Devil appeared before him.

The Devil said to the lawyer, 'I have a proposition for you. You can win every case you try, for the rest of your life. Your clients will adore you, your colleagues will be in awe of you, and you will make incredible sums of money. All I want in exchange is your soul, your wife's soul, your children's souls, the souls of your parents, grandparents, and parents-in-law, and the souls of all of your friends and law partners.'

The lawyer thought about this for a moment, then asked, 'So, what's the catch?'

A Final Note

Oliver was in the hospital, near death, so the family sent for his pastor.

As the pastor stood beside the bed, Oliver's frail condition grew worse, and he motioned frantically for something to write on.

The pastor lovingly handed him a pen and piece of paper, and Oliver used his last ounce of strength to scribble a note.

Then he died.

The pastor thought it best not to look at the note just then, so he slipped it into his jacket pocket.

Several days later, at the funeral, the pastor delivered the eulogy. He realized that he was wearing the same jacket that he'd worn the day Oliver died. 'You know' he said, 'Oliver handed me a note just before he died. I haven't read it, but knowing Oliver, I'm sure there's a word of inspiration there for us all."

He unfolded the note and read aloud, 'You're standing on my oxygen tube!'

Caught In A Flood

A religious man is on top of a roof during a great flood. A man comes by in a boat and says "get in, get in!" The religious man replies "no I have faith in God, he will grant me a miracle."

Later the water is up to his waist and another boat comes by and the man tells him to get in again. He responds that he has faith in God and God will give him a miracle. With the water at about chest high, another boat comes to rescue him, but he turns down the offer again cause "God will grant him a miracle."

With the water at chin high, a helicopter throws down a ladder and they tell him to get in, mumbling with the water in his mouth, he again turns down the request for help for the faith of God.

He arrives at the gates of heaven with broken faith and says to Peter, "I thought God would grand me a miracle and I have been let down."

St. Peter sighs and responds, "I don't know what you're complaining about, we sent you three boats and a helicopter."

A New Pet

A lonely man decides life would be more fun if he had a pet.

So he went to the pet store and told the owner that he wanted to buy an unusual pet.

After careful consideration he finally bought a talking centipede, which came in a little white box to use for his house.

He took the box back home, found a good location for the box, and decided he would start off by taking his new pet to church with him.

So he asked the centipede in the box, "Would you like to go to church with me today? We will have a good time."

But there was no answer from his new pet.

This bothered him a bit, but he waited a few minutes and then asked him again.

"How about going to church with me and receive blessings?"

But, again, there was no answer from his new friend and pet.

So he waited a few minutes more, thinking about the situation.

He decided to ask him one more time; this time putting his

face up against the centipede's house and shouting, "Hey in there! Would you like to go to church with me and learn about the Lord???"

A little voice came out of the box, "I heard you the first time! I'm putting my shoes on."

Sunday School

A Sunday School teacher of small children was concerned that his students might be a little confused about Jesus Christ because of the Christmas season's emphasis on His birth. He wanted to make sure they understood that the birth of Jesus occurred a long time ago, that He grew up, etc. So he asked his class, 'Where is Jesus today?'

Kieron raised his hand and said, 'He's in heaven.'

Davey was called on and answered, 'He's in my heart.'

Paulie, waving his hand furiously, blurted out, 'I know! I know! He's in our bathroom!'

The whole class got very quiet, looked at the teacher, and waited for a response. The teacher was completely at a loss for a few very long seconds. He finally gathered his wits and asked Paulie how he knew this. And Paulie said

'Well every morning, my father gets up, bangs on the bathroom door, and yells 'Jesus Christ, are you still in there?'

God's Promise

A woman had a serious disease and she was taken to the hospital. That night she prayed and asked God if she was going to die. And God said, 'don't worry about it. You have 50 years, 7 months, and 4 days to live.'

Greatly encouraged, she recovered quickly. And she figure that since she had so long to live, she would really live it up. So before she left the hospital, she had a face lift, a breast augmentation, and a tummy tuck. And just for good measure, she cut her hair and changed its color.

The day she left the hospital, she was hit by an ambulance and killed. Standing before God, she asked, 'Why did this happen when You told me I had over 50 years to live?'

And God said, 'Oops, sorry! I didn't recognize you'

Water Into Wine?

A priest is stopped by the police for speeding. The policeman smells wine on the priest's breath, and says, 'Sir, have you been drinking?'

The priest says, 'Just water officer.'

The policeman replies, 'Then why do I smell wine?'

And the minister answers, 'Good grief, He's done it again!'

The Box

A little girl was in church with her mother when she started feeling ill. 'Mommy,' she said, 'can we leave now?'

'No,' her mother replied.

'Well, I think I have to throw up!'

'Then go out the front door and around to the back of the church and throw up behind a bush.'

After about a minute, the little girl returned to her seat.

'Did you throw up?' Mom asked.

'Yes.'

'How could you have gone all the way to the back of the church and returned so quickly?'

'I didn't have to go outside, Mommy. There's a box next to the front door that says, 'For the Sick'.'

The Loch Ness Monster

An atheist was spending a quiet day fishing when suddenly his boat was attacked by the Loch Ness monster. In one quick movement, the beast tossed him and his boat high into the air. Then it opened its mouth to swallow him up.

As the man sailed head over heels, he cried out, "Oh, my God! Help me!"

At once, the ferocious attack scene froze in place, and as the atheist hung in mid-air, a booming voice came down from the clouds, "I thought you didn't believe in Me!"

'Come on God, give me a break!' the man pleaded. 'two minutes ago I didn't believe in the Loch Ness monster either!'

The Affair

These three men show up at the Pearly Gates simultaneously. Peter asks the first one how he died. The man says, "Well, for some time now, I've thought my wife was having an affair, I thought that every day on her lunch break she'd bring her lover home to our 25th floor apartment. So today I was going to come home and catch them. Well, I got there and busted in and immediately began searching for this guy. My wife was half naked and yelling at me as I searched the entire apartment. But, damn it, I couldn't find him! Just as I was about to give up, I happened to glance out onto the balcony and noticed that there was a man hanging off the edge by his fingertips! The nerve of that guy to think he could hide from me! Well, I ran out there and promptly stomped on his fingers until he fell to the ground. But, wouldn't you know it, he landed in some bushes that broke his fall, and he didn't die. In a rage, I went back inside to get the first thing I could get my hands on to throw at him. And oddly enough, the first thing I could grab was the refrigerator. I unplugged it, pushed it out onto the balcony and heaved it over the side. It plummeted 25 stories and crushed him! The excitement of the moment was so great that right after that I had a heart attack and died almost instantly."

Peter turns to the second man and says, 'And how did you die?'

The man says, 'You're not gonna believe this. I was out on the balcony of my 26th floor apartment doing my daily exercises when I got a little carried away and accidentally fell over the side! Luckily however, I was able to catch myself by my fingertips on the balcony directly beneath mine. When all of a sudden this crazy man comes running out of his apartment and starts cussing and stomping on my fingers! Well, of course I fell. I hit some trees and bushes on the way down which broke my fall. As I'm laying there face up on the ground, completely unhurt, I see the man push his refrigerator, of all things, over the ledge and it falls directly on top of me and kills me!'

Peter turns to the third man and says, 'And how did you die?'

The man says, 'OK. Picture this. I'm naked inside a refrigerator'

The Secretary

During a recent Christian meeting, a SECRETARY rushed in and shouted, 'Fire! Fire!'

The METHODISTS gathered in the corner and prayed.

The BAPTISTS cried, 'Where is the water?'

The LUTHERANS posted a notice on the door declaring the fire was evil.

The ROMAN CATHOLICS passed the plate to cover the damage.

THe JEWS posted a symbol on the door hoping the fire would pass.

The CONGREGATIONALISTS shouted, 'Every man for himself.'

The FUNDAMENTALISTS proclaimed, 'It's the vengeance of God.'

The EPISCOPALIANS formed a procession and marched out.

The CHRISTIAN SCIENTISTS concluded there was no fire.

The PRESBYTERIANS appointed a chair person who was to appoint a committee to look into the matter and submit a written report.

The PENTACOSTALS bound the spirit of combustion

The AMISH formed a bucket brigade.

The SECRETARY grabbed a fire extinguisher and put out the fire

A Good Deed

A guy just died and he's at the gates of Heaven, waiting to be admitted, while St. Peter is leafing through this Big Book to see if the guy is worthy. St. Peter goes through the Book several times, furrows his brow and says to the guy, 'You know, I can't see that you ever did anything really bad in your life, but you never did anything really good either. If you can point to even one really good deed you're in.'

The guy thinks for a moment and says, 'Yeah, there was this one time when I was driving down the highway and saw a giant group of Bikers assaulting this poor girl. I slowed down my car to see what was going on and sure enough, there they were, about 50 of 'em abusing this terrified young woman. Infuriated, I got out of my car, grabbed a tire iron out of my trunk, and walked up to the leader of the gang, a huge guy with a studded leather jacket and a chain running from his nose to his ear. As I walked up to the leader, the Biker Gang formed a circle around me. So, I ripped the leader's chain off his face and smashed him over the head with the tire iron. Layed him out. Then I turned and yelled at the rest of them, 'Leave this poor innocent girl alone! You're all a bunch of sick, deranged animals! Go home before I teach you all a lesson in pain!'

St. Peter, impressed, says, 'Really? When did this happen?'

'Oh, about two minutes ago.'

The Monk

There was a man who was fed up with modern society, and decided to become a Monk.

He checked out a number on monasteries and chose one he liked. The only reservation he had with it was he had to take a vow of silence and could only say two words every ten years.

He took the vow and began his first ten years of service without saying a word. At the end of ten long years he was brought before the head of the monastery and was asked what two works he would like to say.

His response was 'FOOD BAD' And that was it for another long, long, ten years, until he was once again allowed to say another two words. After twenty years he was brought before the head of the monastery and was asked what two words he would like to say.

His response was 'BED HARD' and that was it for another long, long, long, ten years, until he was once again allowed to say another two words. After thirty years he was brought before the head of the monastery and asked what two words he would like to say.

His response was 'I QUIT.'

The head man answered back 'You might as well. You've done nothing but complain since you've been here'

Arthritis

A man who smelled like a brewery flopped onto the bus seat next to a Catholic priest. The man's tie was stained and askew; His face and collar were smeared with lipstick; and a half-empty bottle of booze was sticking out of his pocket. The man opened his newspaper and began reading, while the priest sat there in silence and considered what to say. After a few minutes, the drunk turned to the priest and said, 'Say, Padre, what causes arthritis?' Sensing an opportunity to make a point, he replied, 'Mister, it's caused by loose living, drinking, running with loose women, and a total disregard for others.'

'Well, I'll be darned!' Muttered the drunk, and went back to his paper.

After the priest had thought a few minutes about what he'd said, he nudged the man and said, 'Mister, I apologize. I shouldn't have come on so strong. How long have you had arthritis?'

'Oh I don't", replied the man. "I was just reading here in the paper that the pope does.'

A Priest And A Nun

A priest and a nun are lost in a snowstorm. After a while, they come upon a small cabin. Being exhausted, they prepare to go to sleep. There is a stack of blankets and a sleeping bag on the floor but only one bed.

Being a gentleman, the priest says, 'Sister, you sleep on the bed. I'll sleep on the floor in the sleeping bag.'

Just as the priest, zipped up in the bag, is beginning to fall asleep, the nun says, 'Father, I'm cold.'

He unzips the sleeping bag, gets up, gets a blanket and puts it on her.

Once again, he gets into the sleeping bag, zips it up and starts to drift off to sleep when the nun once again says, 'Father, I'm still very cold.'

He unzips the bag, gets up again, puts another blanket on her and gets into the sleeping bag once again.

Just as his eyes close, she says, 'Father, I'm so cold.'

This time, he remains there and says, 'Sister, I have an idea. We're out here in the wilderness where no one will ever know what happened. Let's pretend we're married.'

The nun says, 'That's fine by me.'

To which the priest yells out, 'Get up and get your own stupid blanket!'

Where Is God?

Two brothers are terrible trouble makers. They are always breaking things, stealing things, lying, and making all kinds of general trouble. The parents have tried everything to get the boys to change, to no avail. Finally, out of options, they ask their pastor if he can help. He says he will talk to the boys, but only one at a time. The parents drop off the youngest and go home, promising to return to get him soon. The boy sits in a chair across from the pastor's desk and they just look at each other.

Finally, the Pastor says, 'Where is God?'

The boy just sits there and doesn't answer.

The pastor begins to look stern and loudly says, 'Where is God?'

The little boy shifts in his seat, but still doesn't answer.

The pastor is starting to get angry at the boy's refusal to converse and practically shouts 'Where is God?'

To the pastor's surprise, the little boy jumps up out of his chair and runs out of the office.

The boy leaves the church and runs home, up the stairs and into his brother's room. He shuts the door, 'We're in big trouble. God's missing and they think we did it!'

Don't Do it!

As I was walking across a bridge one day, I saw a man standing on the edge, about to jump off. I immediately ran over and said "Stop! Don't do it!"

'Why shouldn't I?' he said.

I said, 'Well, there's so much to live for!'

'Like what?'

'Well ... are you religious or atheist?'

'Religious.'

'Me too! Are you Christian or Jewish?'

'Christian.

"Me too! Are you Catholic or Protestant?"

"Protestant."

"Me too! Are you Episcopalian or Baptist?"

"Baptist."

"Wow! Me too! Are you Baptist Church of God or Baptist Church of the Lord?"

"Baptist Church of God."

"Me too! Are you Original Baptist Church of God, or are you Reformed Baptist Church of God?"

"Reformed Baptist Church of God."

"Me too! Are you Reformed Baptist Church of God, reformation of 1879, or Reformed Baptist Church of God, reformation of 1915?"

"Reformed Baptist Church of God, reformation of 1915!"

To which I said, "Die, heretic scum!" and pushed him off

Money To The Church

A well-worn one dollar bill and a similarly distressed twenty dollar bill arrived at a Federal Reserve Bank to be retired. As they moved along the conveyor belt to be burned, they struck up a conversation.

The twenty dollar bill reminisced about its travels all over the county. "I've had a pretty good life," the twenty proclaimed. "Why I've been to Las Vegas and Atlantic City, the finest restaurants in New York, performances on Broadway, and even a cruise to the Caribbean."

"Wow!" said the one dollar bill. "You've really had an exciting life!"

"So tell me," says the twenty, "where have you been throughout your lifetime?"

The one dollar bill replies, "Oh, I've been to the Methodist Church, the Baptist Church, the Lutheran Church ...."

The twenty dollar bill interrupts, "What's a church?"

Up To The Monastery

There is a story about a monastery in Europe perched high on a cliff several hundred feet in the air.

The only way to reach the monastery was to be suspended in a basket which was pulled to the top by several monks who pulled and tugged with all their strength.

Obviously the ride up the steep cliff in that basket was terrifying. One tourist got exceedingly nervous about half-way up as he noticed that the rope by which he was suspended was old and frayed.

With a trembling voice he asked the monk who was riding with him in the basket how often they changed the rope.

The monk thought for a moment and answered "Whenever it breaks."

Taxi Driver

A priest and a taxi driver both died and went to heaven. St. Peter was at the Pearly gates waiting for them.

'Come with me', said St. Peter to the taxi driver.

The taxi driver did as he was told and followed St. Peter to a mansion. It had anything you could imagine from a bowling alley to an olympic size pool.

'Wow, thank you', said the taxi driver.

Next, St. Peter led the priest to a rugged old shack with a bunk bed and a little old television set.

'Wait, I think you are a little mixed up', said the priest. 'Shouldn't I be the one who gets the mansion? After all I was a priest, went to church every day, and preached God's word.'

'Yes, that's true. But during your sermons people slept. When the taxi driver drove, everyone prayed.'

Confession

Pat and Mike were walking down the street, when they came to the church, Pat says, 'Mike, you wait here, I'm going to run in for confession, it's been a long time'.

Pat enters the confessional and says,' Father forgive me, I have sinned with a married woman'.

The priest asks, 'was it Mrs Murphy'? 'no, Father', was the reply.

'Was it Mrs O'Boyle'? Again the reply was 'No, Father'.

'Was it Mrs. O'Grady'? Pat said, Father, I'll not be telling you the lady's name!

So the priest told him to say two Hail Mary's for each time he had sinned with the woman.

Back on the street, Mike said, 'Well, how did you do'? Pat said, 'Just fine, I kept me mouth shut and got 3 new prospects'!

A Preacher's Final Wish

An old preacher was dying. He sent a message for his banker and his lawyer, both church members, to come to his home.

When they arrived, they were ushered up to his bedroom. As they entered the room, the preacher held out his hands and motioned for them to sit on each side of the bed. The preacher grasped their hands, sighed contentedly, smiled, and stared at the ceiling. For a time, no one said anything.

Both the banker and lawyer were touched and flattered that the preacher would ask them to be with him during his final moments. They were also puzzled; the preacher had never given them any indication that he particularly liked either of them. They both remembered his many long, uncomfortable sermons about greed, covetousness, and avaricious behaviour that made them squirm in their seats.

Finally, the banker said, "Preacher, why did you ask us to come?"

The old preacher mustered up his strength and then said weakly, "Jesus died between two thieves, and that's how I want to go."

Dental Care

This minister just had all of his remaining teeth pulled and new dentures were being made.

The first Sunday, he only preached 10 minutes.

The second Sunday, he preached only 20 minutes.

But, on the third Sunday, he preached 1 hour 25 minutes.

When asked about this by some of the congregation, he responded this way.

The first Sunday, my gums were so sore it hurt to talk.

The second Sunday, my dentures were hurting a lot.

The third Sunday, I accidentally grabbed my wife's dentures... and I couldn't stop talking!

Blind Man

A Nun was taking a shower one day and she heard the door bell ring, she yelled "Who is it?"

And the person ringing the door bell yelled, "I'm the blind man."

So the Nun got out of the shower and wrapped her hair in a towel, she didn't bother putting a towel around herself because the person behind the door was blind.

She opened the door and said, "What do you want?", and the man said, "I'm here to check your blinds."

Taking A Bullet

The two thousand member Baptist church was filled to overflowing capacity one Sunday morning. The preacher was ready to start the sermon when two men, dressed in long black coats and black hats entered thru the rear of the church.

One of the two men walked to the middle of the church while the other stayed at the back of the church. They both then reached under their coats and withdrew automatic weapons.

The one in the middle announced, "Everyone willing to take a bullet for Jesus stay in your seats!"

Naturally, the pews emptied, followed by the choir. The deacons ran out the door, followed by the choir director and the assistant pastor.

After a few moments, there were about twenty people left sitting in the church. The preacher was holding steady in the pulpit.

The men put their weapons away and said, gently, to the preacher, "All right, pastor, the hypocrites are gone now. You can start the service now."

A Long War

It was about a month ago when a man in Amsterdam felt that he needed to confess, so went to his priest:

"Forgive me Father, for I have sinned. During WWII I hid a refugee in my attic."

"Well," answered the priest, "that's not a sin."

"But I made him agree to pay me 20 Gulden for every week he stayed."

"I admit that wasn't good, but you did it for a good cause."

"Oh, thank you, Father; that eases my mind. I have one more question..."

"What is that, my son?"

"Do I have to tell him the war is over?"

Religious Dogs?

A minister is walking down the street one day, and sees a boy playing with newborn puppies. "Boy, those puppies are a beautiful gift from God. Praytell, what religion are they?"

"Oh, they're Christian puppies, sir." "Glorious! Have a blessed day." The minister goes on his way.

A few weeks later, the same minister is walking down the same street, this time with some fellows from his church. "We have to stop at this boy's house so you can see his puppies. It's adorable, he says they're Christian."

The come to his house, and once again, the boy is outside playing with his puppies. "Little boy, would you mind telling my friends here what religion your puppies are?"

"Sure thing, mister. They don't have a religion, they're atheists."

"What?! You just told me a few weeks ago that they're Christian puppies?"

"Well sir, they were, but they've opened their eyes."

Travelling In Style

A man arrives at Heaven and Michael explains to him how some things work.

"We will provide everything you need here but your mode of transportation is based on how faithful you were in marriage."

The man is satisfied to see that he is given a Volvo. While driving to his new home he sees one of his friends who also arrived that day parked on the side of the road crying in his Aston Martin.

"Why are you crying?! You've earned an Aston Martin for your marital faithfulness!" he says.

His friend looks up and explains, "Yeah, but I just saw my wife on a skateboard!"

Naughty Father

Three nuns were talking. The first nun said, "I was cleaning the father's room the other day and do you know what I found? A bunch of pornographic magazines!"

"What did you do?" the other nuns asked. "Well, of course I threw them all in the trash."

The second nun said, "Well, I can top that. I was in the father's room putting away the laundry and I found a bunch of condoms."

"Oh my," gasped the other nuns.

"What did you do?" they asked.

"I poked holes in all of them," she replied.

The third nun said, "Oh sh#%."

The End Is Near

A local priest and a pastor were fishing on the side of the road. They thoughtfully made a sign saying, "The end is near! Turn yourself around now before it's too late!" and showed it to each passing car.

One driver who drove by didn't appreciate the sign and shouted at them, "Leave us alone, you religious nuts!"

All of a sudden they heard a big splash, looked at each other, and the priest said to the pastor, "You think maybe we should have just said 'Bridge Out' instead?"

Watch Out For The Ducks!

Three women die together in an accident and go to heaven. When they get there, St. Peter says, "We only have one rule here in heaven ... don't step on the ducks."

So they enter heaven, and sure enough, there are ducks all over the place. It is almost impossible not to step on a duck, and although they try their best to avoid them, the first woman accidentally steps on one. Along comes St. Peter with the ugliest man she ever saw.

St. Peter chains them together and says, "Your punishment for stepping on a duck is to spend eternity chained to this ugly man!"

The next day, the second woman accidentally steps on a duck, and along comes St. Peter, who doesn't miss a thing, and with him is another extremely ugly man. He chains them together with the same punishment as the first woman.

The third woman has observed all this and, not wanting to be chained for all eternity to an ugly man, is very, very careful where she steps. She manages to go months without stepping on any ducks, but one day St. Peter comes up to her with the most handsome man she has ever laid eyes on ...very tall, tan, muscular, and with good hair.

St. Peter chains them together without saying a word. The woman remarks, "I wonder what I did to deserve being chained to you for all of eternity?" And the guy says, "Well, I don't know what you did, but I stepped on a duck."

Forrest, Forrest Gump

The day finally arrived: Forrest Gump dies and goes to Heaven. He is at the Pearly Gates, met by St. Peter himself.

St. Peter says, "Well, Forrest, it's certainly good to see you. We have heard a lot about you. I must inform you that the place is filling up fast, and we've been administering an entrance examination for everyone. The test is short and you have to pass before you can get into heaven.

      1)What days of the week begin with the letter T?
      2) How many seconds are there in a year?
      3) What is God's first name?"

Forrest says, "Well, the first one -- how many days in the week begin with the letter 'T'? That one's easy. That'd be Today and Tomorrow."

The Saint's eyes open wide and he exclaims, "Forrest, that's not what I was thinking, but ..... I'll give you credit for that answer."

"How about the second one?" asks St. Peter. "How many seconds in a year?"

"Now that one's harder," says Forrest, "but I thunk and thunk and guess the only answer can be twelve."

Astounded, St. Peter says, "Twelve? Twelve? Forrest, how in Heaven's name could you come up with twelve seconds in a year?"

"Shucks, there's gotta be twelve: January 2nd, February 2nd, March 2nd."

"Hold it," interrupts St. Peter. "I see where you're going with this, and I'll have to give you credit for that one, too. Let's go on with the next and final question."

"Can you tell me God's first name?"

"Sure" Forrest replied, "its Andy."

"Andy?!" exclaimed an exasperated and frustrated St. Peter. "Ok, I can understand how you came up with your answers to my first two questions, but just how in the world did you come up with the name of Andy as the first name of God?"

"That was the easiest one of all," Forrest replied.

"ANDY WALKS WITH ME, ANDY TALKS WITH ME, ANDY TELLS ME I AM HIS OWN."

Adam And Eve

After spending time with Eve, Adam was walking in the Garden with God. Adam told God how much the woman meant to him and how blessed he felt to have her. Adam began to ask questions about her.

Adam: Lord, Eve is beautiful. Why did you make her so beautiful?

God: So you would always want to look at her.

Adam: Lord, her skin is so soft. Why did you make her skin so soft?

God: So you would always want to touch her.

Adam: She always smells so good. Lord, why did you make her smell so good?

God: So you would always want to be near her.

Adam: That's wonderful Lord, and I don't want to seem ungrateful, but why did you make her so stupid?

God: So she would love you.

Hell Improvements

An engineer dies and reports to the pearly gates. St. Peter checks his dossier and says, "Ah, you're an engineer -- you're in the wrong place."

So, the engineer reports to the gates of hell and is let in. Pretty soon, the engineer gets dissatisfied with the level of comfort in hell, and starts designing and building improvements. After awhile, they've got air conditioning and flush toilets and escalators, and the engineer is a pretty popular guy.

One day, God calls Satan up on the telephone and says with a sneer, "So, how's it going down there in hell?"

Satan replies, "Hey, things are going great. We've got air conditioning and flush toilets and escalators, and there's no telling what this engineer is going to come up with next."

God replies, "What??? You've got an engineer? That's a mistake -- he should never have gotten down there; send him up here."

Satan says, "No way." I like having an engineer on the staff, and I'm keeping him."

God says, "Send him back up here or I'll sue."

Satan laughs uproariously and answers, "Yeah, right. And just where are YOU going to get a lawyer?"

Which Room?

A man died and went straight down to hell. The devil greeted him and gave him a guided tour of the place. He told the man that there were three rooms he could choose from in which to spend eternity. The first room was full of flames so hot the man couldn't even breathe. He told the devil that there was no way he was choosing that room. So they moved on.

The next room they came to was full of people who were being beaten and tortured. It looked so painful the man could not watch. He told the devil he definitely didn't want that room, and they moved on.

The last room they came to was full of people who were just sitting around drinking coffee and relaxing. The only thing was that they were standing around in about two feet of poop. The man looked for a while and then told the devil this room would be all right.

The devil gestured for him to sit down. He did, sipped his coffee and felt really pleased with his choice. After a few minutes, a voice came over the loudspeaker and said, "Break time is over! Back on your heads!"

The King Of Pop

A little kid asks his father, "Daddy, is God a man or a woman?"

"Both son. God is both."

After a while the kid comes again and asks, "Daddy, is God black or white?"

"Both son, both."

The child returns a few minutes later and says, "Daddy, is Michael Jackson God?"

What The Devil?

One Sunday morning, everyone in one bright, beautiful, tiny town got up early and went to the local church.

Before the services started, the townspeople were sitting in their pews and talking about their lives, their families, etc. Suddenly, Satan appeared at the front of the church. Everyone started screaming and running for the front entrance, trampling each other in a frantic effort to get away from evil incarnate.

Soon everyone was evacuated from the church, except for one elderly gentleman who sat calmly in his pew, not moving... seemingly oblivious to the fact that God's ultimate enemy was in his presence. Now this confused Satan a bit, so he walked up to the man and said, "Don't you know who I am?"

The man replied, "Yep, sure do."

Satan asked, "Aren't you afraid of me?"

"Nope, sure ain't," said the man.

Satan was a little perturbed at this and queried, "Why aren't you afraid of me?"

The man calmly replied, "Been married to your sister for over 48 years."

Young Man

A young man once asked God how long a million years was to him.

God replied, "A million years to me is just like a single second to you."

The young man asked God what a million dollars was to him.

God replied, "A million dollars to me is just like a single penny to you."

Then the young man got his courage up and asked, "God, can I have a penny?"

God smiled and replied, "Certainly, just a second."

Three Priests

Two priests died at the same time and met Saint Peter at the Pearly Gates.

St. Peter said, "I'd like to get you guys in now, but our computer is down. You'll have to go back to Earth for about a week, but you can't go back as priests. So what else would you like to be?"

The first priest says, "I've always wanted to be an eagle, soaring above the Rocky Mountains."

"So be it," says St. Peter, and off flies the first priest.

The second priest mulls this over for a moment and asks, "Will any of this week 'count', St. Peter?"

"No, I told you the computer's down. There's no way we can keep track of what you're doing."

"In that case," says the second priest, "I've always wanted to be a stud."

"So be it," says St. Peter, and the second priest disappears.

A week goes by, the computer is fixed, and the Lord tells St. Peter to recall the two priests. "Will you have any trouble locating them?" He asks.

"The first one should be easy," says St. Peter., "He's somewhere over the Rockies, flying with the eagles. But the second one could prove to be more difficult."

"Why?" asks the Lord. "He's on a snow tire, somewhere in North Dakota."

Ordained

Twelve priests were about to be ordained. The final test was for them to line up in a straight row, totally naked, while a beautiful, big-breasted nude model danced before them.

Each priest had a small bell attached to his penis. They were told that anyone whose bell rang when the nude model danced in front of them would not be ordained, because he had not reached a state of spiritual purity.

The beautiful model danced before the first candidate, with no reaction. She proceeded down the line with the same response from all the priests until she got to the final priest.

As she danced, his bell began to ring so loudly that it flew off and fell clattering to the ground. Embarrassed, he took a few steps forward and bent over to pick up the bell...

Then all the other bells started to ring.

Mother-In-Law

A Bible group study leader says to his group, "What would you do if you knew you only had four weeks left before the great Judgment Day?"

A gentleman says, "I would go out into my community and minister the Gospel to those that have not yet accepted the Lord into their lives."

"Very good!" says the group leader.

One lady speaks up and says enthusiastically, "I would dedicate all of my remaining time to serving God, my family, my church, and my fellow man with a greater conviction."

"That's wonderful!" the group leader comments.

One gentleman in the back finally speaks up loudly and says, "I would go to my mother-in-laws house for the four weeks."

The group leader asks, "Why your mother-in-law's home?"

"Because that will make it the longest four weeks of my life!"

An Ad Campaign

Wilson runs a nail factory and decides his business needs a bit of advertising. He has a chat with a friend who works in marketing, and he offers to make a television ad for Wilson's Nails.

"Give me a week," says the friend, "and I'll be back with a tape."

A week goes by and the marketing executive comes to see Wilson. He puts a cassette in the video and presses play.

A Roman soldier is busy nailing Jesus to the cross. He turns to face the camera and says with a grin, "Use Wilson's Nails, they'll hold anything."

Wilson goes mad, shouting, "What is the matter with you? They'll never show that on television. Give it another try, but no more Romans crucifying Jesus!"

Another week goes by and the marketing man comes back to see Wilson with another tape. He puts it in the machine and hits play. This time the camera pans out from a Roman standing with his arms folded to show Jesus on the cross. The Roman looks up at him and says, "Wilson's Nails, they'll hold anything."

Wilson is beside himself. "You don't understand. I don't want anything with Jesus on the cross! Now listen, I'll give you one last chance. Come back in a week with an advertisement that I can broadcast."

A week passes and Wilson waits impatiently. The marketing executive arrives and puts on the new video. A naked man with long hair, gasping for breath, is running across a field. About a dozen Roman soldiers come over the hill, hot on his trail.

One of them turns to the camera and says, "If only we had used Wilson's Nails!"

Bible Class

In Sunday school, Sister Mary asked the class: "What part of the body goes to heaven first?"

In the back of the class, nasty Billy waved his hand frantically, but Sister Mary, suspecting a wrong answer, turned to another child. "Yes, Susan?"

"The heart goes to heaven first because that's where God's love lives."

"Excellent," said Sister Mary, "and you, Charlotte?"

"The soul, Sister Mary, because that's the part that lives beyond death."

"Very good, Charlotte," said the Sister, as she noticed Billy's hand still waving in desperation."

"OK, Billy, what do you think?"

"It's the feet that go first, Sister, the feet."

"That's a strange answer Billy. Why the feet?"

Billy answered, "Because I saw my mom with her feet up in the air, shouting, 'God, I'm coming, I'm coming!'"

The Post Office

A little boy was waiting for his mother to come out of the grocery store.

As he waited, he was approached by a man who asked, "Son, can you tell me where the post office is?"

The little boy replied, "Sure, just go straight down the street a couple of blocks and turn to your right."

The man thanked the boy kindly and said, "I'm the new pastor in town, and I'd like for you to come to church on Sunday. I'll show you how to get to Heaven."

The little boy replied with a chuckle, "How to get to Heaven? You don't even know how to get to the post office!"

Schooling

Angela was nearing 60 and was in her final year of teaching.

She was a devout Christian who missed teaching from the Bible.

Because she was worried at how little her class knew about religion, Angela decided she was going to disregard the new regulations and teach some religion.

She told her class that she would run a contest. She would give $50 to whoever could tell her who was the greatest man who ever lived.

Immediately Moishe began to wave his hand, but Angela ignored him in favor of those in her Sunday school class.

As she went around the room, Angela was disappointed with the answers she got.

Jane, her best scholar, picked Noah because he saved all the animals.

Others said, "I think the greatest man who ever lived was Alexander the Great because he conquered the whole world." and "I think it was Thomas Edison, because he invented the light bulb."

Finally, she called on Moishe who still had his hand in the air.

"I think the greatest man who ever lived was Jesus Christ."

said Moishe.

Angela was shocked but still gave him the $50 reward.

As she did so, she said, "Well, Moishe, I'm very surprised that you should be the only one with the right answer. How come?"

"Well, to tell you the truth," Moishe replied as he pocketed the money, "I think it was Moses, but business is business.

Jesus Saves

Jesus and Satan were having an on-going argument about who was better on the computer. They had been going at it for days, and frankly God was tired of hearing all the bickering.

Finally fed up, God said, 'THAT'S IT! I have had enough. I am going to set up a test that will run for two hours, and from those results, I will judge who does the better job.'

So Satan and Jesus sat down at the keyboards and typed away.

They moused.

They faxed.

They e-mailed.

They e-mailed with attachments.

They downloaded.

They did spreadsheets!

They wrote reports.

They created labels and cards.

They created charts and graphs.

They did some genealogy reports

They did every job known to man.

Jesus worked with Heavenly efficiency and Satan was faster than hell.

Then, ten minutes before their time was up, lightning suddenly flashed across the sky, thunder rolled, rain poured, and, of course, the power went off..

Satan stared at his blank screen and screamed every curse word known in the underworld.

Jesus just sighed.

Finally the electricity came back on, and each of them restarted their computers. Satan started searching frantically, screaming: 'It's gone! It's all GONE! 'I lost everything when the power went out!'

Meanwhile, Jesus quietly started printing out all of his files from the past two hours of work..

Satan observed this and became irate.

'Wait!' he screamed. 'That's not fair! He cheated! How come he has all his work and I don't have any?'

God just shrugged his shoulders and said, "JESUS SAVES"

Jesus Is Watching You

A burglar broke into a home and was looking around.

He heard a soft voice say, "Jesus is watching you".

Thinking it was just his imagination, he continued his search. Again the voice said "Jesus is watching you".

He turned his flashlight around and saw a parrot in a cage. He asked the parrot if he was the one talking and the parrot said, "yes."

He asked the parrot what his name was and the parrot said, "Moses."

The burglar asked, "what kind of people would name a parrot Moses?"

The parrot said, "the same kind of people who would name their German Shepherd Jesus".

Anyone For Golf?

The Pastor woke up Sunday morning and realizing it was an exceptionally beautiful and sunny early spring day, decided he just had to play golf. So.... he told the associate pastor that he was feeling sick and convinced him to preach for him that day. As soon as the associate pastor left the room, the Pastor headed out of town to a golf course about forty miles away. This way he knew he wouldn't accidentally meet anyone he knew from his church.

Setting up on the first tee, he was alone. After all, it was Sunday morning and everyone else was in church!

At about this time, Saint Peter leaned over to the Lord while looking down from heaven and exclaimed, "You're not going to let him get away with this, are you?"

The Lord sighed, and said, "No, I guess not."Just then he hit the ball and it shot straight towards the pin, dropping just short of it, rolled up and fell into the hole. It was a 420 yard hole in one!

Saint Peter was astonished. He looked at the Lord and asked, "Why did you let him do that?"

The Lord smiled and replied, "Who's he going to tell?"

Ten Things You Never Hear In Church

Hey! It's my turn to sit in the front pew.

I was so enthralled, I never noticed your sermon went 25 minutes over time.

Personally I find witnessing much more enjoyable than golf.

I've decided to give our church the $500 a month I used to send to TV evangelists.

I volunteer to be the permanent teacher for the Junior High Sunday School class.

Forget the denominational minimum salary, let's pay our pastor so he/she can live like we do.

I love it when we sing hymns I've never heard before!

Since we're all here, let's start the service early.

Pastor, we'd like to send you to this Bible seminar in the Bahamas.

Nothing inspires me and strengthens my commitment like our annual stewardship campaign!

I couldn't find space to park outside. Praise God

Driving Along

The Pope had just finished a tour of the East Coast and was taking a limousine to the airport. Having never driven a limo, he asked the chauffeur if he could drive for awhile.

Well, the chauffeur didn't have much of a choice, so the chauffeur climbs in the back of the limo and the Pope takes the wheel. The Pope proceeds to hop on Route 95 and starts accelerating to see what the limo could do. He gets to about 90 miles per hour and, WHAM, there are the blue lights of our friendly State Police in his mirror.

He pulls over and the trooper comes to his window. Seeing who it was the trooper says "just a moment please I need to call in."

The trooper radio's in and asks for the chief. He tells the chief "I've got a REALLY important person pulled over and I need to know what to do."

The chief replies "Who is it, not Ted again ?"

The trooper says,"No, even more important."

The chief replies, "It's the Governor, is it?"

The trooper replies "No, even more important."

"It's isn't the President is it?"

"No, more important", replies the trooper.

"Well who the heck is it then!?" screams the chief.

"I don't know" says the trooper. "But he's got the Pope as a chauffeur!"

Christianity According To Kids

In the first book of the Bible, Guinessis, God got tired of creating the world, so he took the Sabbath off.

Adam and Eve were created from an apple tree.

Noah's wife was called Joan of Ark.

Noah built an ark, which the animals come on to in pears.

Lot's wife was a pillar of salt by day, but a ball of fire by night.

Samson was a strongman who let himself be led astray by a Jezebel like Delilah.

Samson slayed the Philistines with the axe of the Apostles.

Moses led the Hebrews to the Red Sea, where they made unleavened bread which is bread without any ingredients.

The Egyptians were all drowned in the dessert.

Afterwards, Moses went up on Mount Cyanide to get the ten ammendments.

The first commandment was when Eve told Adam to eat the apple.

The fifth commandment is to humor thy father and mother.

The seventh commandment is thou shalt not admit adultery.

Moses died before he ever reached Canada.

Then Joshua led the Hebrews in the battle of Geritol.

The greatest miracle in the Bible is when Joshua told his son to stand still and he obeyed him.

David was a Hebrew king skilled at playing the liar. He fought with the Finklesteins, a race of people who lived in Biblical times.

Solomon, one of David's sons, had 300 wives and 700 porcupines.

When Mary heard that she was the mother of Jesus, she sang the Magna Carta.

When the three wise guys from the east side arrived, they found Jesus in the manager.

Jesus was born because Mary had an immaculate contraption.

St. John, the blacksmith, dumped water on his head.

Jesus enunciated the Golden Rule, which says to do one to others before they do one to you.

He also explained, "a man doth not live by sweat alone."

It was a miracle when Jesus rose from the dead and managed to get the tombstone off the entrance.

The people who followed the Lord were called the 12 decibels.

The epistles were the wives of the apostles.

One of the opossums was St. Matthew who was also a taximan.

St. Paul cavorted to Christianity. He preached holy acrimony, which is another name for marriage.

A Christian should have only one spouse. This is called monotony

The Hotel Is Full

A Jewish lady named Mrs. Rosenberg many years ago was stranded late one night at a fashionable resort - one that did not admit Jews. The desk clerk looked down at his book and said, "Sorry, no room. The hotel is full."

The Jewish lady said, "But your sign says that you have vacancies."

The desk clerk stammered and then said curtly, "You know that we do not admit Jews. Now if you will try the other side of town..."

Mrs. Rosenberg stiffened noticeable and said, "I'll have you know I converted to your religion."

The desk clerk said, "Oh, yeah, let me give you a little test. How was Jesus born?"

Mrs. Rosenberg replied, "He was born to a virgin named Mary in a little town called Bethlehem."

"Very good," replied the hotel clerk. "Tell me more."

Mrs. Rosenberg replied, "He was born in a manger."

"That's right," said the hotel clerk. "And why was he born in a manger?"

Mrs. Rosenberg said loudly, "Because a jerk like you in the hotel wouldn't give a Jewish lady a room for the night!"

The Parrot

A very religious woman went into the local pet shop to buy a parrot for company. She selected a beautiful bird, but the pet store owner said he didn't think she'd be happy with this particular parrot because he had belonged to a salty old sailor who used very bad language.

She replied that she knew with love and care she could break the bird of his bad habits and have a wonderful companion.

Well, the bird was not to be broken of his blue language and the woman had to hide him in the spare bedroom every time she had visitors. Finally, in desperation she told the bird she was going to put him in the freezer for 10 minutes every time he used bad language. Sure enough in just a couple of minutes the bird let out a string of obcenities. She put him in the freezer with him hollering and yelling his head off. After just a minute or two it got very quiet.....afraid that something bad had happened to the bird, she opened the door.

Out stepped the parrot, shivering and most pleasantly and politely he said "excuse my prior behavior, madam. I regret any dismay I may have caused you and promise never to use improper language again."

Well, the woman was thrilled to hear these promises and was about to say so when the bird interrupted to say "by the way, madam, what's the chicken in for?"

The Donkey

A preacher wanted to raise money for his church and on being told that there was a fortune in horse racing, decided to purchase one and enter it in the races. However at the local auction, the going price for horses was so high that he ended up buying a donkey instead. He figured that since he had it, he might as well go ahead and enter it in the races. To his surprise, the donkey came in third! The next day the local paper carried this headline:

"PREACHER'S ASS SHOWS!"

The preacher was so pleased with the donkey that he entered it in the race again, and this time it won. The paper read:

"PREACHER'S ASS OUT IN FRONT"

The Bishop was so upset with this kind of publicity that he ordered the preacher not to enter the donkey in another race. The paper headline read:

"BISHOP SCRATCHES PREACHER'S ASS"

This was too much for the Bishop, so he ordered the preacher to get rid of the donkey. The preacher decided to give it to a nun in a nearby convent. The paper headline the next day read:

"NUN HAS BEST ASS IN TOWN"

The Bishop fainted. He informed the nun that she would have to get rid of the donkey, so she sold it to a farmer for

$10.00. Next day the headline read:

"NUN SELLS ASS FOR $10.00"

This was too much for the Bishop, so he ordered the nun to buy back the donkey, lead it to the plains where it could run wild and free. Next day, the headline in the paper read:

"NUN ANNOUNCES HER ASS IS WILD AND FREE"

The Bishop was buried the next day.

A Quick Email

An Illinois man who left the snowballed streets of Chicago for a vacation in Florida. His wife was on a business trip and was planning to meet him there the next day. When he reached his hotel, he decided to send his wife a quick e-mail.

Unable to find the scrap of paper on which he had written her e-mail address, he did his best to type it

in from memory. Unfortunately, he missed one letter and his note was directed instead to an elderly preacher's wife, whose husband had passed away only the day before. When the grieving widow checked her e-mail, she took one look at the monitor, let out a piercing scream, and fell to the floor dead.

At the sound, her family rushed into the room and saw this note on the screen:

Dearest Wife,
Just got checked in. Everything prepared for your arrival tomorrow. Your Loving Husband.

P.S.: Sure is hot down here.

Grandma's Note

The other day I went to the local religious book store
where I saw a "Honk if you really love Jesus" bumper
sticker. I bought it and put it on the back bumper of my car
and I'm really glad I did. What an uplifting experience
followed.

I was stopped at the light of a busy intersection, just lost in
thought
about the Lord, and didn't notice that the light had
changed. That bumper sticker really worked! I found lots
of people who love Jesus. Why, the guy behind me started
to honk like crazy. He must really love the Lord because
pretty soon he leaned out his window and yelled, "Jesus
Christ!" as loud as he could.

Why, it was like a football game with him shouting, "Go,
Jesus Christ, Go"! Everyone else started honking too, so I
leaned out my window and waved and smiled to all those
loving people. There must have been a guy from Florida
back there because I could hear him
yelling something about a sunny beach, and I saw him
waving in a funny way with only his middle finger stuck up
in the air.

I had recently asked my two grandsons what that meant.
They kind of squirmed, looked at each other, giggled and
told me that it was the Hawaiian good luck sign, so I
leaned out the window and gave him the good luck sign
back. A couple of the people were so caught up in the joy
of the moment that they got out of their cars and were
walking towards me. I bet they wanted to pray, but just

then I noticed that the light had changed, and I stepped on the gas.

It's a good thing I did, because I was the only car to get across the intersection. I looked back at them standing there. I leaned out the window, gave them a big smile, and held up the Hawaiian Good Luck sign as I drove away.
Praise
the Lord for such wonderful folks!

Love ya all,
Grandma

A Religious Debate

Several centuries ago, the Pope decreed that all the Jews had to leave Italy. There was, of course, a huge outcry from the Jewish community, so the Pope offered a deal. He would have a religious debate with a leader of the Jewish community. If the Jewish leader won the debate, the Jews would be permitted to stay in Italy. If the Pope won, the Jews would have to leave.

The Jewish community met and picked an aged Rabbi, Moishe, to represent them in the debate. Rabbi Moishe, however, could not speak Latin and the Pope could not speak Yiddish. So it was decided that this would be a "silent" debate.

On the day of the great debate, the Pope and Rabbi Moishe sat opposite each other for a full minute before the Pope raised his hand and showed three fingers.

Rabbi Moishe looked back and raised one finger.

Next, the Pope waved his finger around his head.

Rabbi Moishe pointed to the ground where he sat.

The Pope then brought out a communion wafer and chalice of wine.

Rabbi Moishe pulled out an apple. With that, the Pope stood up and said, "I concede the debate. This man has bested me. The Jews can stay."

Later, the Cardinals gathered around the Pope, asking him

what had happened.

The Pope said, "First I held up three fingers to represent the Trinity. He responded by holding up one finger to remind me that there was still one God common to both our religions. Then I waved my finger around me to show him that God was all around us. He responded by pointing to the ground to show that God was also right here with us. I pulled out the wine and the wafer to show that God absolves us of our sins. He pulled out an apple to remind me of original sin. He had an answer for everything. What could I do?"

Meanwhile, the Jewish community crowded around Rabbi Moishe, asking what happened. "Well," said Moishe, "first he said to me, 'You Jews have three days to get out of here.' So I said to him, 'Up yours'. Then he tells me the whole city would be cleared of Jews. So I said to him, 'Listen here Mr. Pope, the Jews ... we stay right here!"

"And then?" asked a woman.

"Who knows?" said Rabbi Moishe. "We broke for lunch."

What Was Jesus?

THREE PROOFS THAT JESUS WAS JEWISH
He went into his father's business
He lived at home until he was 33
He was sure his Mother was a virgin, and his Mother was
sure he was God

THREE PROOFS THAT JESUS WAS IRISH
He never got married
He was always telling stories
He loved green pastures

THREE PROOFS THAT JESUS WAS PUERTO RICAN
His first name was Jesus
He was bilingual
He was always being harassed by the authorities

THREE PROOFS THAT JESUS WAS ITALIAN
He talked with his hands
He had wine with every meal
He worked in the building trades

THREE PROOFS THAT JESUS WAS BLACK
He called everybody "brother"
He liked Gospel
He couldn't get a fair trial

THREE PROOFS THAT JESUS WAS A CALIFORNIAN
He never cut his hair
He walked around barefoot
He started a new religion

THREE PROOFS THAT JESUS WAS A WOMAN

He had to feed a crowd, at a moments notice, when there was no food
He kept trying to get the message across to a bunch of men who just didn't get it
Even dead, he had to get up because there was more work for him to do.

Confession 2

A priest was called away for an emergency. Not wanting to leave the confessional unattended, he called his rabbi friend from across the street and asked him to cover for him. The rabbi told him he wouldn't know what to say, but the priest told him to come on over and he'd stay with him for a little bit and show him what to do. The rabbi comes, and he and the priest are in the confessional.

In a few minutes, a woman comes in and says, "Father, forgive me for I have sinned.

The priest asks, "What did you do?"

The woman says, "I committed adultery."

Priest: "How many times?"

Woman: "Three times."

Priest: "Say two Hail Marys, put $5 in the box, and go and sin no more."

A few minutes later, a man enters the confessional. He says, "Father, forgive me for I have sinned."

Priest: "What did you do?"

Man: "I committed adultery."

Priest: "How many times?"

Man: "Three times."

Priest: "Say two Hail Marys, put $5 in the box, and go and sin no more."

The rabbi tells the priest that he thinks he's got it so the priest leaves.

A few minutes later, another woman enters and says, "Father, forgive me for I have sinned."

Rabbi: "What did you do?"

Woman: "I committed adultery."

Rabbi: "How many times?"

Woman: "Once."

Rabbi: "Go do it two more times. We have a special this week, three for $5."

On Vacation

Two priests were going to Hawaii on vacation and decided that they would make this a real vacation by not wearing anything that would identify
them as clergy.

As soon as the plane landed, they headed for a store and bought some really outrageous shorts and Aloha shirts, sandals, sunglasses, etc. The next morning, they went to the beach, dressed in their tourist gear and were sitting on beach chairs, enjoying cocktails, the sunshine and the scenery when a drop dead gorgeous redhead in a tiny bikini came walking straight toward them.

They couldn't help but stare and when she passed them she turned to them, smiled and said, "Good morning Father Murphy. Good Morning Father Doyle," nodding and addressing each of them individually, then passed on by.

They were both stunned. How in the world did she recognize them as priests?

The next day they went back to the store, bought even more outrageous outfits. These outfits were so loud, you could hear them before you even saw them. Again, they settled on the beach in their chairs to enjoy the sunshine.

After a while, the same gorgeous redhead, wearing a string bikini this time, came walking toward them again. Again, she approached them and greeted them individually, "Good Morning Father Murphy. Good Morning Father Doyle," and started to walk away.

One of the priests couldn't stand it and said, "Just a minute young lady. Yes we are priests, and proud of it, but I have to know, how in the world did you know?"

"Oh Father, don't you recognize me? I'm Sister Rachael!"

A Halo And Wings

A lady dies and goes to heaven. She arrives at the pearly gates and is greeted by Saint Peter. There are a few people waiting, so she strikes up a conversation with him. Just then, she hears a blood curdling scream!

"What was that?" she asks.

"Oh, don't worry about that," says Saint Peter, "it's just someone getting a hole drilled in their head so they can be fitted for their halo."

A few seconds later, she hears another agonized scream, this one even more terrible than the one before.

"What was that?!" she asked anxiously.

"Oh, don't worry," says Saint Peter soothingly, "It's just someone getting holes drilled in their back so they can be fitted for their wings."

The lady starts to back away.

"Where are you going?" asks Saint Peter. "I think I'll go downstairs, if it's all the same to you," says the lady.

"But you can't go there," says the saint, "You'll be raped and sodomized!"

"It's OK," says the lady, "I've already got the holes for that."

A Bad Copy

A new monk arrived at the monastery. He was assigned to help the other monks in copying the old texts by hand. He noticed, however, that they were copying copies, not the original books. The new monk went to the head monk to ask him about this. He pointed out that if there were an error in the first copy, that error would be continued in all of the other copies.

The head monk said, "We have been copying from the copies for centuries, but you make a good point, my son." The head monk went down into the cellar with one of the copies to check it against the original.

Hours later, nobody had seen him, so one of the monks went downstairs to look for him. He heard a sobbing coming from the back of the cellar and found the old monk leaning over one of the original books, crying. He asked what was wrong.

"The word is 'celebrate'," said the head monk.

Daily Bread

A guy from Tyson Foods arranges to visit the Pope. After receiving the papal blessing he whispers, "Your Eminence, we have a deal for you. If you change The Lord's Prayer from 'give us this day our daily bread....' to 'give us this day our daily chicken....' then we will donate $500 million dollars to the Church".

The Pope responds saying, "That is impossible. The Prayer is the Word of the Lord and it must not be changed."

"Well," says the Tyson man, "we are prepared to donate $1 billion to the Church if you change the Lord's Prayer from 'give us this day our daily bread....' to 'give us this day our daily chicken....'"

Again the Pope replies "That is impossible. The Prayer is the Word of the Lord and it must not be changed."

Finally, the Tyson guy says, "This is our last offer. We will donate $5 billion to the church if you change the Lord's Prayer from 'give us this day our daily bread....' to 'give us this day our daily chicken....'" and he leaves.

The next day the Pope meets with the College of Cardinals to say that he has good news and some bad news.

"The good news is that the Church has come into $5 billion."

"The bad news is that we are losing The Wonderbread Account"

Close To God

86 year old Morris went for his annual physical. All of his tests came back with great results. Dr. Cohen said, "Morris everything looks great physically. How are you doing mentally, emotionally and are you at peace with yourself, and have a good relationship with God?"

Morris replied, "God and me are tight. We are so close that when I get up in the middle of the night, *poof* . . . the light goes on when I go to the bathroom and then *poof* the light goes off!"

"Wow," commented Dr. Cohen, "That's incredible!"

A little later in the day Dr. Cohen called Morris's wife. "Becky," he said, "Morris is just fine. Physically he's great. But I had to call because I'm in awe of his relationship with God. Is it true that he gets up during the night and *poof* the light goes on in the bathroom and then *poof* the light goes off?"

Becky replied, "The darn fool! . . . He's peeing in the fridge again!"

Collection Money

A priest, rabbi and televangelist were playing their usual Wednesday round of golf, and started discussing their weekly collections. Specifically, they started to compare how they decided what portion of the collection to keep for themselves and what portion to give to God.

The rabbi explains: "I draw a circle around myself and toss the money in the air. Whatever lands in the circle I keep for myself. Whatever lands outside the circle, I give to God."

The priest then adds: "I use a similar method, except that whatever lands in the circle I give to God, and whatever lands outside the circle I keep for my personal needs."

The televangelist then proclaims: "I also use the same method. Except, that I toss the money in the air and I figure that whatever God wants, he can take."

The Provider

A young woman brings home her fiancee to meet her parents. After dinner, her mother tells her father to find out about the young man. The father invites the fiancee to his study for a drink.

"So what are your plans?" the father asks the young man.

"I am a Torah scholar," he replies.

"A Torah scholar. Hmmm," the father says. "Admirable, but what will you do to provide a nice house for my daughter to live in, as she's accustomed to?"

"I will study," the young man replies, "and God will provide for us."

"And how will you buy her a beautiful engagement ring, such as she deserves?" asks the father.

"I will concentrate on my studies," the young man replies, "God will provide for us."

"And children?" asks the father. "How will you support children?"

"Don't worry, sir, God will provide," replies the fiancee.

The conversation proceeds like this, and each time the father questions, the young idealist insists that God will provide.

Later, the mother asks, "How did it go, Honey?"

The father answers, "He has no job and no plans, but the good news is he thinks I'm God."

A Lesson In Elasticity

A teacher asked her clase, "What's the strechiest substance in the World?"

Up jumped little Tommy, "I know this one sir."

"Yes Tommy, what would say is the most stretchy substance in the world?"

"Human skin sir." said Tommy.

"I don't think so, but what makes you say that it's human skin Tommy?"

"It says so in the Bible sir."

"I can't recall reading this in the Bible Tommy. Perhaps you could quote it for us." said the teacher.

"Yes sir. It says " . . . and Jesus tied his Ass to a tree and walked 3 miles into Jerusalem."

The Afterlife

A couple made a deal that whoever died first, they would come back and inform the other of the afterlife. Her biggest fear was there was no heaven. After a long life the husband was the first to go and true to his word he made contact.

Mary... Mary....

Is that you Fred?

Yes, I have come back like we agreed.

What is it like?

Well, I get up in the morning, I have sex, I have breakfast, I have sex, I bath in the sun, then I have sex-twice, I have lunch, then sex pretty much all afternoon, supper, then sex till late at night, sleep then start all over again.

Oh Fred you surely must be in heaven.

"Hell no, I'm a rabbit in Arkansas."

Finding Jesus

A drunk stumbles along a baptismal service on Sunday afternoon down by the river.

He proceeds to walk down into the water and stand next to the preacher. The minister turns and notices the old drunk and says, "Mister, are you ready to find Jesus?"

The drunk looks back and says, "Yes, Preacher, I sure am."

The minister then dunks the fellow under the water and pulls him right back up. "Have you found Jesus?" the preacher asked.

"Nooo, I didn't!" said the drunk.

The preacher then dunks him under for quite a bit longer, brings him up and says, "Now, brother, have you found Jesus?"

"Noooo, I have not, Reverend."

The preacher in disgust holds the man under for at least 30 seconds this time, brings him out of the water and says in a harsh tone, "My God, man, have you found Jesus yet?"

The old drunk wipes his eyes and says to the preacher, "Are you sure this is where he fell in?"

Dear Pastor

Dear Pastor, I know God loves everybody but He never met my sister.
Yours sincerely, Arnold. Age 8, Nashville.

Dear Pastor, Please say in your sermon that Peter Peterson has been a
good boy all week. I am Peter Peterson. Sincerely, Pete. Age 9,
Phoenix

Dear Pastor, My father should be a minister. Every day he gives us a
sermon about something. Robert, Page 11, Anderson

Dear Pastor, I'm sorry I can't leave more money in the plate, but my
father didn't give me a raise in my allowance. Could you have a sermon
about a raise in my allowance? Love, Patty. Age 10, New Haven

Dear Pastor, My mother is very religious. She goes to play bingo at
church every week even if she has a cold. Yours truly, Annette. Age 9,
Albany

Dear Pastor, I would like to go to heaven someday because I know my
brother won't be there. Stephen. Age 8, Chicago

Dear Pastor, I think a lot more people would come to your

church if you
moved it to Disneyland. Loreen. Age 9. Tacoma

Dear Pastor, I liked your sermon where you said that good health is more
important than money but I still want a raise in my allowance.
Sincerely, Eleanor. Age 12, Sarasota

Dear Pastor, Please pray for all the airline pilots. I am flying to
California tomorrow. Laurie. Age 10, New York City

Dear Pastor, I hope to go to heaven some day but later than sooner.
Love, Ellen, age 9. Athens

Dear Pastor, Please say a prayer for our Little League team. We need
God's help or a new pitcher. Thank you. Alexander. Age 10, Raleigh

Dear Pastor, My father says I should learn the Ten Commandments. But I
don't think I want to because we have enough rules already in my
house. Joshua. Age 10, South Pasadena

Dear Pastor, Who does God pray to? Is there a God for God? Sincerely,
Christopher. Age 9, Titusville

Dear Pastor, Are there any devils on earth? I think there may be one in my class. Carla. Age 10, Salina

Dear Pastor, I liked your sermon on Sunday. Especially when it was
finished. Ralph, Age 11, Akron

Dear Pastor, How does God know the good people from the bad people? Do
you tell Him or does He read about it in the newspapers? Sincerely,
Marie. Age 9, Lewiston

Hypnotising

A local preacher was dissatisfied with the small amount in the collection plates each Sunday. Someone suggested to him that perhaps he might be able to hypnotize the congregation into giving more. "And just how would I go about doing that?" he asked.

"It's very simple. First you turn off the air conditioner so that the auditorium is warmer than usual. Then you preach in a monotone. Meanwhile, you dangle a watch on a chain and swing it in a slow arc above the lectern and suggest they put 20 dollars in the collection plate."

So the very next Sunday, the reverend did as suggested, and lo and behold the plates were full of 20 dollar bills. Now, the preacher did not want to take advantage of this technique each and every Sunday. So therefore, he waited for a couple of weeks and then tried his mass hypnosis again.

Just as the last of the congregation was becoming mesmerized, the chain on the watch broke and the watch hit the lectern with a loud thud and springs and parts flew everywhere.

"Crap!" exclaimed the pastor.

It took them a week to clean up the church.

The Kid's Confession

A couple was making love when all of a sudden there were keys opening the door. The woman said, "Hide! It's my husband!"

The guy jumped into the closet only to hear a voice saying, "It sure is dark in here."

The guy replied, "Who is that?"

The voice replied, "I am the son and I am going to tell!"

The guy said, "No! Please! I'll give you $20."

The kid replied, "No. I am going to tell!"

The guy begged, "Please! I only have $40 and you can have it if you don't tell."

The kid took the money and once the husband went to the store, the guy was able to escape.

The next day the kid went to his mom to ask for the bike he had always wanted.

Mom replied, "Son, we don't have the money."

The kid quickly answered, "I have $40!"

Suprised, his mother asked where he got the money, but the child would not answer.

Angry, the mother took the kid by the ear, marched him down to the church and tossed him into the confession booth.

Upset, the kid shouted, "Hey! It's dark in here!"

The preacher in the confessional replied, "Oh don't start that again!"

A New Pope

Every time a new Pope is elected, there are a whole lot of rituals and ceremonies that have to be gone through, in accordance with tradition.

Well there's one tradition that very few people know about. Shortly after the new Pope is enthroned, the Chief Rabbi seeks an audience. He is shown into the Pope's presence, whereupon he presents him with a silver tray bearing a velvet cushion. On top of the cushion is an ancient, shriveled parchment envelope. The Pope symbolically stretches out his arm in a gesture of rejection. The Chief Rabbi then retires, taking the envelope with him and does not return until the next Pope is elected.

John Paul II was intrigued by this ritual, whose origins were unknown to him. He instructed the best scholars of the Vatican to research it, but they came up with nothing. When the time came and the Chief Rabbi was shown into his presence, he faithfully enacted the ritual rejection but, as the Chief Rabbi turned to leave, he called him back.

"My brother," the Holy Father whispered, "I must confess that we Catholics are ignorant of the meaning of this ritual enacted for centuries between us and you, the representative of the Jewish people. I have to ask you, what is it all about?"

The Chief Rabbi shrugs and replies: "But we have no more idea than you do. The origin of the ceremony is lost in the mists of ancient history."

The Pope said: "Let us retire to my private chambers and

enjoy a glass of wine together, then, with your agreement, we shall open the envelope and discover at last the secret." The Chief Rabbi agreed.

Fortified in their resolve by the wine, they gingerly pried open the parchment envelope and with trembling fingers, the Chief Rabbi reached inside and extracted a folded sheet of similarly ancient paper. As the Pope peered over his shoulder, he slowly opened it. They both gasped with shock.

It was the check for the Last Supper.

At The Pearly Gates

St. Peter stood at the Pearly Gates, waiting for the incoming. He saw Jesus walking by and caught his attention. "Jesus, could you mind the gate while I go do an errand?"

"Sure," replied Jesus. "What do I have to do?"

"Just find out about the people who arrive. Ask about their background, their family, and their lives. Then decide if they deserve entry into Heaven."

"Sounds easy enough. OK."

So Jesus waited at the gates while St. Peter went off on his errand.

The first person to approach the gates was a wrinkled old man. Jesus summoned him to the examination table and sat across from him. Jesus peered at the old man and asked, "What was it you did for a living?"

The old man replied, "I was a carpenter."

Jesus remembered his own earthly existence and leaned forward. "Did you have any family?" he asked.

"Yes, I had a son, but I lost him."

Jesus leaned forward some more. "You lost your son? Can you tell me about him?"

"Well, he had holes in his hands and feet."

Jesus leaned forward even more and whispered, "Father?"

The old man leaned forward and whispered, "Pinocchio?"

God Made Us

Grandpa and granddaughter were sitting talking when she asked, "Did God make you, Grandpa?"

"Yes, God made me," the grandfather answered.

A few minutes later, the little girl asked him, "Did God make me too?"

"Yes, God made you," the older man answered.

For a few minutes, the little girl seemed to be studying her grandpa, as well as her own reflection in a nearby mirror, while her grandfather wondered what was running through her mind.

At last she spoke up.

"You know, Grandpa," she said, "God's doing a lot better job lately.

Healing The Blind

Poor little Herbie. Since his birth, poor blind Herbie had never seen the light of day. One day at bedtime, his mother told him that the next day would be a very special one. If he prayed extra hard to Jesus, he'd be able to see when he woke up the next morning.

Eagerly, Herbie crouched down on his knees beside his bed and put his hands together. For hours, he prayed and prayed to Jesus.

The next morning Herbie's mother came into his room and gently woke him from his sleep.

"Well Herbie, open your eyes and you'll know that Jesus answered your prayers."

Little Herbie slowly opened his eyes, only to cry out, "Mother! Mother! I STILL CAN'T SEE!"

"I know, dear," said his mother. "APRIL FOOL!"

Bill Gates

Bill Gates dies and heads up to the pearly gates.

Saint Peter meets him there and says, "Well, you've led an... interesting life, Bill. To be perfectly honest, we're not quite sure which place to send you. So we're going to let you decide.'

Gates swallows nervously and says, 'okay'.

St. Peter snaps his fingers and they are instantly transported to a beach with a party. There's lots of alcohol, tons of food, rock music and topless women playing volleyball, and many other 'naughty' behaviors going on.

Gates says,'Hey, is this heaven? It's great!'

St. Peter says,'No, this is Hell. Let me show you what Heaven is like.'

He snaps his fingers again and they are instantly transported to a peaceful cloudy space. There's a soft breeze and angels and people are floating around playing harps and worshiping the glory and light that is God.

Gates says,'Well, this is... nice. But, given a choice, I guess I'll take Hell.'

St. Peter says,'You got it,' and snaps his fingers.

Gates is instantly imbedded in molten lava where his skin is flayed off in unspeakable agony. All around him he can hear demonic laughter and the screams of the damned.

Bill Gates looks up and shouts,'Hey, it wasn't like this! Where's the beach?Where's the Women? Where's the food and fun?'

Just then, satan appears in front of him, in all his horned maliciousness. Satan grins and says, 'Oh I'm sorry Bill, but that was the just the demo version.'

Mistaken Identity

A man was being tailgated by a stressed out woman on a busy boulevard, when suddenly, the light turned yellow, just in front of him. He did the right thing and stopped, even though he could have beaten the red light by accelerating through the intersection.

The tailgating woman hit the roof, and the horn, screaming in frustration as she missed her chance to get through the intersection.

As she was still in mid-rant, she heard a tap on her window and looked up into the face of a very serious police officer. The officer ordered her to exit her car with her hands up. He took her to the police station where she was searched, finger printed, photographed, and placed in a holding cell.

After several hours, a policeman approached the cell and opened the door. She was escorted back to the booking desk where the arresting officer was waiting with her personal effects.

He said, "I'm very sorry for this mistake. You see, I pulled up behind your car while you were blowing your horn, flipping off the guy in front of you, and cussing a blue streak at him. I noticed the 'Choose Life' license plate, the 'What Would Jesus Do?' bumper sticker, the 'Follow Me to Sunday-School' bumper sticker, and the chrome-plated Christian fish emblem on the trunk. Naturally, I assumed you had stolen the car."

Made in the USA
Middletown, DE
18 June 2019